Locked In and Out

OBJECTS TALK BACK

About This Book Series

In collaboration with the Ethnologisches Museum and the Museum für Asiatische Kunst of the Staatliche Museen zu Berlin, the Stiftung Humboldt Forum im Berliner Schloss invited the writer Priya Basil to curate a series of events and books: *Objects Talk Back*.

Every year, Priya Basil asks two writers to engage with an object of their choice—either from the exhibited collection or from the museums' storage depot.

The project represents a new curatorial practice (complementing ongoing provenance research) characterised by transparency and dialogue regarding the collections in the Humboldt Forum, the complex history of its location and entanglements with contemporary global issues. The aim is to investigate the provenance history of the objects while simultaneously engaging in a direct dialogue with people biographically connected to the countries of origin, thereby fostering international multivocality and transforming museum practices.

Priya Basil

Locked In and Out

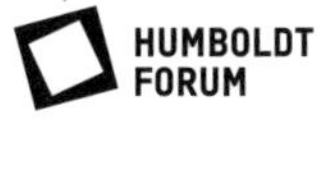

DIAPHANES

Humboldt Forum
Modern building behind reconstructed Baroque palace façades
Construction period: 2012–2020
Address: Schloßplatz, 10178 Berlin

The Humboldt Forum was established in 2002 by a resolution of the German Bundestag. Four partner institutions are responsible for its programming: the Stiftung Humboldt Forum im Berliner Schloss; the Stiftung Preußischer Kulturbesitz with the Ethnologisches Museum and the Museum für Asiatische Kunst of the Staatliche Museen zu Berlin; the Stadtmuseum Berlin; and Humboldt University. Additionally, it fosters collaborations with Berlin communities and global partners on an equal basis. Since its opening in summer 2021, the Humboldt Forum has become a vibrant hub for intercultural dialogue and engagement with global issues.

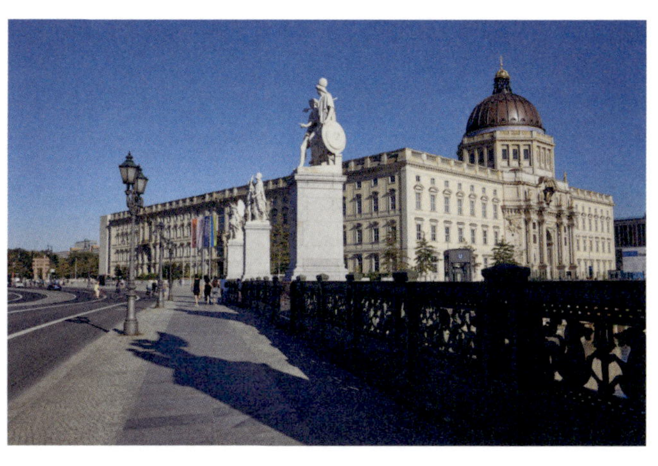

OBJECTS TALK BACK

Objects have voices, which we may not hear. Literature helps us to listen.

Objects Talk Back is a project that asks: what are the possibilities of literature to open up new stories, questions and relations when writers engage with museum archives?

While there are promising currents of change, ethnological museum collections remain tied to violent colonial histories and ongoing practices of domination. Information for most objects is still limited to date of creation or acquisition, place of origin, type of material, collector or donator. Even these details are not always accurate.

The archaeologist Dan Hicks proposes "necrography," a practice of digging into the past to trace the colonial story behind an object.[1] Such an approach may reveal much of value, but also leave one "straining against the limits of the archive," as literary scholar Saidiya Hartman writes.[2]

Colonial archives contain their own prejudices and distortions. Hartman suggests "critical fabulation"—melding history, theory and fiction—"to displace the received or authorized account." Inspired by these ideas, I coined the term "fabulography" for *Objects Talk Back*. In a piece for *British Art Studies*, I describe fabulography as an invitation to work creatively with-from-through gaps, facts and imagination to expand the narrative space around an object.[3] Fabulography involves digging deep, uncovering painful details, but also rising up, celebrating, honouring, reconnecting.

Since 2021, two writers are invited each year to explore collections of the Ethnological Museum and the Museum of Asian Art, both part of the Staatliche Museen zu Berlin. The writers encounter objects displayed in the Humboldt Forum, Berlin and also those stored in the museum depots. They select an object, and respond however they wish—through fiction, poetry, narrative non-fiction, multi-media texts. Later, they present the finished work at a live event in the Humboldt Forum.

Now, objects talk back in a book series as well, affirming Hartman's appeal "to consider stories as a form of compensation, perhaps the only kind we will ever receive."[4]

Priya Basil

1 Dan Hicks, "Necrography: Death-Writing in the Colonial Museum," *British Art Studies*, Issue 19, 2021: https://doi.org/10.17658/issn.2058-5462/issue-19/conversation | 2 Saidiya Hartman, "Venus in Two Acts," *Small Axe* (Indiana University) 12, no. 2 (2008): https://muse.jhu.edu/search?action=browse&limit=publisher_id:3 (accessed March 9, 2024) | 3 Priya Basil, "Writing to Life," *British Art Studies*, Issue 19, 2021: https://www.britishartstudies.ac.uk/issues/issue-index/issue-19/death-writing-in-the-colonial-museums (accessed March 9, 2024) | 4 Hartman, "Venus in Two Acts."

Hartmut Dorgerloh

Preface

Teekesselchen is the German term for a game that helps children learn about homonyms, words with multiple meanings. For Priya Basil, who grew up in an English-speaking environment, it might have been known as "tea kettle," though such things are rarely that straightforward. Words can not only have multiple meanings—they can also be understood differently, heard incorrectly, or outright misinterpreted.

Who speaks, when, about what, with what intention, in what language, from what position? These questions have become increasingly important in a world overwhelmed by text, non-stop posts, pervasive propaganda and frequent misinformation.

Priya Basil, a British-Indian writer and activist who grew up in Kenya, studied in the UK and now lives in Berlin, is particularly intrigued by the German *Teekesselchen* word *Schloss*, which means both "castle" or "palace" and "lock." Her film essay *Locked In and Out, EingeSCHLOSSen / AusgeSCHLOSSen*, which premiered at the opening of the Humboldt Forum in 2020, explores the controversies surrounding the reconstruction of the Berliner Schloss (Berlin Palace) and the collections on display there, all too many of which are linked to colonial violence and domination. The word *Schlüssel*, or "key," is central to her in this context, for every *Schloss*—whether a palace or a lock—requires a key. But who holds the key, and how is it used?

Priya Basil's response is that we can all act as keys by not staying outside the door, by not closing ourselves off and withholding criticism, but by opening ourselves up, being accessible and not excluding others.

Objects Talk Back is the name of the program that Priya Basil has been curating for the Humboldt Forum since 2020 and whose results are being published, starting with this volume. But can objects, things on display in museums, really speak, answer, or even contradict? Yes, if we learn to listen to them anew. To this end—and in the spirit of her book *Hospitality* (2019), which intertwines political and philosophical questions with individual memories—Priya Basil invites authors from all over the world. Her aim is precisely this: to give the objects (nowadays also referred to as "cultural belongings") a voice again, to make them speak, specifically with regard to our questions and our thoughts, so that we can be "keys." We all bring with us our biographical experiences and the memories associated with them, including the objects. For Priya Basil, memories are one of the few things in the world that can be both a *Schlüssel* (key) and a *Schloss* (lock).

Linking the personal with the political and the fictional with the historical is a key theme for Priya Basil, whose novels have been nominated for numerous awards and who writes regularly for *Lettre International* and newspapers such as *DIE ZEIT* and *The Guardian*. She is also a co-founder of Authors for Peace.

During the years when Berlin became her home, the new *Schloss* went up in the center of the city, modeled on the old one and built on a historic site. Even those who had not been actively involved in the post-1990 debates about the reconstruction of Berlin's Hohenzollern Palace and the associated demolition of the East German Palace of the Republic could no longer ignore this "colossal error of a building" (Basil). Coming from Great Britain and unfamiliar with what is often claimed in Germany as a critical confrontation with the country's history, the author wondered how this could happen here. Can a rebuilt *Schloss* become a new venue for art and cultures from all over the world, or is this where the gaps in the official memory politics and dominant historiography become evident, and not just in terms of pervasive German ignorance toward the country's colonial history? For Priya Basil, criticism and distance combine with commitment and creativity—merely complaining is not enough. Tolerating contradictions, accepting criticism, engaging with the history of the site and its exhibits with an open mind, bringing people and perspectives together in all their diversity—these are the challenges that the Humboldt Forum must, and is eager to, confront.

Priya Basil inaugurates this new publication series of the Humboldt Forum with a text that addresses this very challenge and discusses the *Schloss* itself, its architecture, its significance, the controversies and irritations it has provoked, thereby providing the basis and framework for subsequent publications in the series.

In the volumes that will follow, authors selected by Priya Basil and invited by the Humboldt Forum will focus on individual objects of their choice that are displayed or stored here. The encounter with those objects will trigger strong impulses, raise many questions and provoke deep reflection, irrespective of the authors' biographies and backgrounds.

The collaboration with Priya Basil and the other authors is truly a key experience for the Humboldt Forum, for which we, who are responsible for this venue and its program, are profoundly grateful.

We all need these texts, these perspectives, as a set of keys to a better and deeper understanding of this place and its collections, and their relevance to us today. And this is true even when the words have multiple meanings.

Translated from German
by Bram Opstelten

Priya Basil

Locked In and Out

In German the word *Schloss* means a palace, and also a "lock."

In English the word "belonging" means a condition of affinity, a secure relationship to a person, place or thing. It also means "possessions"—as in these are my belongings, your belongings, our belongings.

In 2002, I began living in Berlin and writing my first novel, based on my ancestors who moved across the world in the twentieth century, propelled by the forces of Empire. They went from India to Kenya to Britain, their lives shaped by British colonialism as well as the counter struggles for independence and redress.

In 2002, the German parliament voted in favor of rebuilding a palace from the Prussian era and the

Kaiserreich, periods synonymous with militarism and colonialism.

Back then, I did not know that I would eventually settle down in Berlin. I did not know I would become a German citizen. I did not know that over the coming years the sense of what it means to be German—in Europe, in the world—an understanding necessarily always in flux—would start to shift dramatically, even shake. I did not know that the very idea of who counts as a citizen, who can belong, would be brazenly contested, even in so-called mature democracies, as illiberal currents—nationalistic, racist, misogynistic—currents narrow and exclusionary in every way—swelled in Germany and across the globe.

Some knew: from the start, many parts of civil society, from activists to academia, resisted the building of the Berlin Palace. Their critique catalyzed a long overdue public debate about Germany's pre-Nazi colonial past and how it affects present ideas of belonging. All the while, buildings emblematic of a drive to distort history were—are—being reconstructed or planned in other cities. The New Old Town in Frankfurt am Main, the Frauenkirche in Dresden, the Garrison Church in Potsdam. Such neo-national architecture has enthusiastic backers amongst the far-right—people locked into a fantasy of white supremacy. The reconstructions also have support amongst some conservatives and moderates—people who have perhaps not quite understood what such developments really mean. The Berlin Palace is only the most conspicuous example of a reactionary trend, but it is the most problematic because of its function: to house looted, or dubiously obtained, ethnological objects and simultaneously develop a decolonizing approach to itself, its holdings and its workings with others.

The central question: Can a lock also be a key?

Wait: perhaps we should no longer refer to ethnological "objects"—but rather to "belongings"? It moves us away from the tidy abstraction of "objects," which implies a blankness on which anyone can project, objectify. "Belongings," on the other hand, intricately, inextricably ties up notions of possession, being and longing.

In December 2018, two years after the UK voted to leave the EU and it seemed there might be a hard Brexit, I entered a small ground-floor room in the District Office for Mitte, Berlin. Also there were my husband and the civil servant who had overseen my citizenship application and checked that I had passed my citizenship test. I signed a few final documents and then stood to pledge: "I solemnly declare that I will respect the Constitution and the laws of the Federal Republic of Germany and will refrain from doing anything that could harm them." I can't believe I've got this, I said, clutching my citizenship certificate as we left. "With that you get responsibility for the Holocaust too," my husband said. He went on talking. I didn't hear a thing. I was thinking, he could have waited a bit longer before making that observation. At the same time, I was feeling an awful weight. The past had acquired a different charge: a history I had studied as a guest of sorts had become mine to host. If there is one advantage of the British triumphalist obsession with World War II, it's that the Holocaust features prominently, and therefore, right from my school days, this crime had assumed a pivotal place in my sense of the past and present. Still, the heft of the knowledge had suddenly changed.

Germany's memorial culture after the Holocaust initially appeared to me to cohere around the notion *Wiedergutmachung*—to make good again—through reparation, restitution, remorseful remembrance. This approach seemed exemplary to me, schooled as I was in British jingoism and an unapologetically self-congratulatory take on the past, the imperial glory days. It was in Berlin, a city full of memorials to victims of the Nazi tyranny, that I began to wonder about the nature of public memory in general, but especially in Britain. For years I walked over *Stolpersteine*[1]—commemorative stumbling stones set into cobbled streets—in this country and thought about the other country, Britain, to which I belonged by dint of chance: my birth there, my British passport and all the associated opportunities were mine only because others had suffered, resisted, paid and died as colonial subjects. I thought of that country where there is not a single compulsory school class, let alone a memorial, acknowledging the crimes of its vast, cruel Empire. I was grateful for the contrast Germany offered, for what it revealed to me. But it's also painful to realize you have been cheated by your country, told a false or incomplete history, and also painful to see that you were foolish enough to fall for it.

Wary of being caught out again, I paid particular attention to critiques of Germany's memory culture: to flaws in the *Wiedergutmachung* premise, to those who said some things could never be made good again, those who said some methods of remembrance seemed designed more to assuage German guilt than respond to the actual needs and wishes of a diverse Jewish community. I paid attention to how the memorial landscape of the city gradually extended to include Roma and Sinti, homosexual victims, and those killed in the euthanasia program of the Third Reich. I paid attention to the commemoration of German reunification, noting how the joining of East and West was reified in various ways, even as cultural traces of the East were erased. I paid attention to the crimes of Germany's pre-Nazi colonial past, which were less salient in the public consciousness, less significant on the political agenda, less worthy, so far, of memorials: the genocide from 1904–1908 of around 100,000 Herero and Nama peoples in Namibia; the approximately 250,000 victims of German atrocities in Tanzania, including those who died in the Maji Maji war to oust German colonial forces. There had been no questions related to these latter events in my citizenship test. Glaring gaps in memory, in the willingness to memorialize. Yet, it seemed to me, there was still much to value in the German approach, which had locked a commitment to remembering the Holocaust to the very core of social, political and cultural life. This has been key to some of the better aspects of Germany.

Memory is one of the few things in the world that can be both lock and key. Even if the lock sometimes jammed, stuck fast, kept important things out—I still believed that Germany's practice with this mechanism for holding on to awful lessons from its Nazi past would be a key to opening up ways to deal with its earlier colonial history, key to opening up other ways of relating to the world, to each other. And then came the Berlin Palace.

In 2020, across the world anti-racist movements bring down colonial statues, altering the face of cities, challenging authority—and Germany opens its biggest cultural project of the twenty-first century: a reconstructed imperial palace in the heart of the capital, filled with the ill-gotten belongings of communities all over the world. How could this come to pass? What kind of remembrance culture is this?

The palace stands, on center stage, like a body builder, holding that pose known in the sport as "most muscular"; legs spread, arms raised, everything flexed, not least the sinuous facades, which were recreated almost to the last detail and paid for with private donations to the tune of €100 million. An advert for how class and money can influence the character of public space in democratic Germany even in the twenty-first century. An advert for a very modern form of feudalism that can co-opt €572 million of state funds into serving private minority interests as well as the interests of the ill-informed. The Berlin Palace project was initiated and lobbied for by an association comprised of people who were, presumably, steeped in Germany's memory culture yet nevertheless managed to hold, and try to recreate, an idealized version of its imperial past. So idealized, that nowhere on their website, even on the page citing the arguments against the reconstruction, does the word "colonial" appear to play a role.

Until summer 2020, I had seen the body builder only from a distance, glimpsed the east facade, the "rear lat spread"—less grotesquely sinuous, but equally ominous for its fascist architectural echoes. I had held back from going there, as one intuitively tries to avoid danger. What the threat was I could not quite articulate then. Now I know it was the fear of having to reconsider, once more, a history I had for the most part accepted, the fear of having to face up to my failure, once again, to grasp the scale of its incompleteness. And it was the more painful this time because it was not a case of childish misapprehensions, as with my view of Britain's past. Mine was now the folly of an adult who had critiqued, questioned, paid attention—and still misjudged. Why did I think Germany would be better? Why did I think I would be better?

I have always fallen in love too quickly—with people, places, ideas. My whole adult life I've been training myself not to be too eager, not open up too much too soon, not to believe—but to hold back, wait, doubt. In Germany I fell in love with an idea that was not true, never can be: the society that knows how to remember. *Wieder gut machen.* Make good again. Is that what would be tried with this new aberration? Something that should never have happened would—surely, eventually—be set right. To be clear: this is a different order of error, reconstructing a building is in no way equivalent to constructing a whole architecture of mass murder. But rebuilding the Berlin Palace, renaming it the Humboldt Forum, and then attempting to undo what the palace is from within the place itself strike me as signs of the *Wiedergutmachung* mentality.

And yet, and yet. Even now—is this misguided?—I do not believe the possibility of making good again, setting things right, should be discarded, just better interrogated. Key, in this regard, are the allies we choose, the methods we use. I myself now try to practice what Priyamvada Gopal, in line with many other postcolonial theorists, calls "a sustained unlearning."[2] For me, this means being alert to harmful patterns in my own thoughts and actions; it means listening, staying open, being vulnerable, able to change course, to admit error.

Donna Haraway sums it up well: "decolonizing requires a kind of radical not-knowing, emptying-out, a kind of truly not-knowing, so as to somehow be less stupid."[3]

The Humboldt Forum cannot be allowed to fail, someone said to me. And I wondered: wasn't it already a failure—in that it had come to pass? The state cannot allow it to go down, the person clarified, they can't just close shop and get out; it's too visible, too important, too costly. And I wondered, would the body builder stand the weight of its own expectations, contradictions and obligations; could it handle its own historical doping?

Wait: the courtyard now known as Schlüterhof was originally made during extensions to the Berlin Palace done between 1689 and 1713 on the orders of the Great Elector Frederick who, in 1701, declared himself the first king of Prussia. His father was responsible for establishing the Brandenburg colony Groß-Friedrichsburg, a trading post on the Gold Coast in West Africa, held by the family from 1683 to 1718; from there, up to 30,000 Africans were enslaved and sold to America.

The first time I went within the palace walls, I felt the force field of coloniality, its distorting effect. I saw how some of the newly commissioned artworks were already misshapen, like the sculpture of large letters circling the walls of one room, spelling out the names of all the architects who had been responsible for erecting something on the site over the centuries. Why? I wondered. Why in this macho building would you have more men's names blown up and paraded? Or was that the point? An accusation to emphasize the long line of male dominance? If so, it seemed to me an attempt to mend that only reproduced an ugly trope. I wished for a line of graffiti sprayed roughly in red: *where were all the women?* I wished for meticulous carvings in every wall marking the names of all those who had been exploited or killed to make palaces like this one possible. At the same time, I was aware it might add insult to injury to have such names here. A monument can't be turned into a memorial with mere gestures, especially not when its walls are already inscribed with the names of the biggest private donors to its cause. Questions rang through the empty halls: whose names do we venerate? Whose memory do we honor? Whose lives matter? And the other eternal dilemma: How to engage on these issues without repeating in other ways the violence that has already been done, how to try to repair without inadvertently harming again?

After that visit, I stopped asking myself, "*how could this happen*?" Suddenly, it was perfectly clear: this is a very truthful building, a perfect example of a certain kind of dominance—white, mostly male—that continues very successfully to reproduce itself. The Berlin Palace expresses that dominance in its most confident, entitled form. The building is a Monumental Homage to Coloniality.

The diffuse architecture of coloniality is everywhere—that is to say, our relations to each other continue to be constructed within social, racial, political, juridical and economic realities deformed by the legacies of European colonialism. This architecture may be variously subtle or blatant, more noticed or ignored, but it is omnipresent. The Berlin Palace is coloniality distilled, its essence set in stone. A stone you don't just stumble over, but crash into.

The architecture is disturbing enough, but then there are the collections: thousands upon thousands of belongings with as many stories, deaths, traumas, ruptures, questions. Holding on to such belongings, most of which are the possessions of others from around the world, must now mean holding yourself accountable to the world. The palace juggernaut has locked Germany into a very public reckoning with its pre-Nazi colonial past.

The strangest thing for me is that on this perilous site all my histories collide. On the ground of the monument I understood better the nature of the weight that had settled in me the day I became a German citizen, and which I had been carrying around ever since. It was the weight of wondering how to hold together all the different histories that were now mine without needing to choose between them or have a hierarchy.

The crimes of the British Empire are so heinous, so numerous, I sometimes think I could study that history my whole life and not fathom the full extent of it. Still, there are facts that stand out for me because they overlap in different ways with my biography: the massacre of thousands of Mau Mau rebels who fought for Kenyan independence; the economic plunder of India and the killing of tens of millions of Indians through brute force as well as callous policies in the face of famine; the Balfour Declaration with its implications for Palestine, and later, after the Holocaust, its implications for the state of Israel. Is it possible, as a dual citizen, to keep my British and German colonial histories equally close, to hurt with each without risking an accusation of minimizing one or the other, to see them in relation to each other, to (un-)learn from this particular, personal convergence of the past and the present?

The Humboldt Forum unsettles all sense of

place, all sense of time, forces a repositioning of self within entangled histories that stretch in all directions from the belongings held there. It compels us to acknowledge multiple affinities, dependencies, loyalties, duties—and obliges us to search together for ways of negotiating these.

The Humboldt Forum's architecture and the bulk of the collections combine to create a shocking, harrowing nexus of coloniality. It's hard to imagine anyone would do this deliberately. It's hard to imagine this could happen accidentally. It's hard to know that this is the reality of ethnological museums. Many of the belongings in these places have lain for years in archives—untouched, unseen, unvalued—and still there is reluctance to relinquish them. The excuse of obscure provenance—*we don't know where they came from!*—is no reason not to try to know. Anything else is just a case of what Ariella Aïsha Azoulay calls "*imperial retentiveness*: the ability to retain the outcome of imperial violence as fact, as what is, what one is, and what one has."[4]

Wait: Can we really speak of ethno-logical museums? Might it not be more accurate to say ethno-illogical museums for places that have long propagated racist classifications and hierarchies, turned stolen cultural artefacts into tools for enforcing white domination?

The only option, as more experts in the field are now advocating, is complete restitution of the belongings asked for by their owners, as well as efforts to reconnect with owners who may not be aware of who holds their belongings. And lest we think this a radical, enlightened position, Azoulay reminds us that it is "neither a progressive idea nor 'the most advanced' phase of 'our democracies', so much so that centuries were supposedly required to reach such a point."[5]

A palace is about defensiveness as well as display; palaces kept most people out, held their treasures close yet at the same time showed off to all. This duality pervades the Humboldt Forum, which displays readiness to decolonize and at the same time defends its collections simply through continuing to display them—even if this is supposed to be done in a more reflective, self-critical way.

There's something perverse in how the deliberations on restitution are so drawn out, as if to enable an elaborate display of angst and contrition which give the impression of really caring—for the belongings, for their communities, for due process. In fact, what's really going on is a kind of cover-up of defensiveness, of a conviction in still knowing best, of not believing people can take care of their own belongings.

There's a version of such dualities in me too; in many of us, I guess. I want to display my willingness to question, to change in the face of these challenges, in light of new insights. Yet even as I do, defensiveness crowds my thoughts; nostalgia for things from which I have benefitted, anxiety about what may be lost. Yet, the ebbing hesitation of someone once enchanted by what turned out to be criminal elements in what I took for your-my-our-world culture sits alongside the growing urgency of someone who accepts it is time to unlearn.

Part of what defines public spaces like the Humboldt Forum are the longings of the society to whom, as a state institution, it is ultimately beholden. Like it or not, those of us who live in Germany are locked into the fate of this place. It is a kind of citizenship test that shatters the national frame in which we tend to understand the term "citizen." It rattles assumptions about rights and responsibilities. What does it mean to possess rights that are dependent on the dispossession of others?

Far from healing a wound at the center of the city, as initiators of the palace reconstruction project claim, this edifice brings into stark relief the extent of an injury that stretches from the palace at Schloßplatz, to the Holocaust Memorial at Cora-Berliner-Straße 1, to Wilhelmstraße 92—the site of the former Reich Chancelry, where the Berlin Conference took place in 1884–1885. There, major European powers, including Britain, France, Belgium,

Portugal and Germany, negotiated and formalized claims to territory in Africa. They went on to expand their claims on the continent, and by 1900 European states had stakes on nearly ninety percent of it. The Berlin Conference was the decisive, inaugural blast in what Dan Hicks calls World War Zero:[6] the period from 1884 to 1914, when the European colonial powers brutally subjugated African peoples, exploiting and killing them, stealing their resources and treasures. Today at Wilhelmstraße 92, there is a single, modest memorial board describing the outcome of the conference. The wound is raw, gaping, weeping.

So, what made me enter the palace, knowing all this? I required some reason, something I could hold on to like a rope, tug, twist, tie to other knowledges and experiences. In spring 2020, I was invited to conceptualize and curate a project that would involve bringing together writers and belongings from the collections to see what kinds of narrations could emerge. I felt cautious, but also curious, because it seemed to me that this could offer a chance to challenge the traditional master narrative of the museum, to disrupt the hubristic script that said everything should stay here—for the sake of the world, of course—and we are the most qualified locksmiths. Maybe there's also a presumption in thinking you can step into the machinery of power and change anything. If so, it is a necessary presumption, because power never budges of its own accord.

I imagine a new question on the citizenship test with its standard four multiple-choice answers from which I must pick one:

As a citizen faced with the Humboldt Forum, what are your options?

1. Visit and enjoy
2. Boycott
3. Inner migration
4. Ask questions, and more questions, keep asking even if it hurts

I could tick three of those and justify them elaborately, but I pick number 4.

Those who started working in the Humboldt

Forum, planning the future program while the building was still being completed, had to wear hard hats to enter and move around. I too donned a bright blue one when I went. Walking through the space confirmed what I had intuited from a distance and stated in my concept proposal: the physical building of the Humboldt Forum may be almost ready, one day soon it may even appear "complete," but, in truth, this place could never be "finished": the (re-) building of knowledges, of relationships, of understanding, of repair—to name just a few aspects—all remain perpetually under construction. And the developments, internal and external, had to remain transparent, legible. Narratives are made from processes: every step is part of the story. All processes are imperfect, but if they can be read, they can be improved. I suggested artistic documentation of process as a central part of the project concept I submitted: a means to record achievements, discoveries, misunderstandings, disappointments and failings from all sides—my own included. That is the true nature of a test, after all: to reveal both how much you know and don't know and, perhaps most importantly, to reveal what you are prepared to do with that knowledge.

Still, no matter the methodologies you use, the allies you choose, always, always, with such an institution the concerns remain, the rumblings of conscience, the warnings of allies: Consorting with the enemy! Tainted by association! Compromised! Naïve! Deluded! I hesitate, I want to retreat, to wait until I've unlearned more, until I've learned enough—which means waiting forever. Inner migration is not an effective tool for political insurgency. Boycott can be powerful; my own criticality is sharpened by those who abstain from anything to do with the palace.

I can step away from the Humboldt Forum, but I can't step out of the world: the dilemmas don't go away just because I keep a distance from one version of them. Moreover, I cannot be indifferent to the fact that there are others, amongst them initiators of the palace reconstruction and some members of their Circle of Friends, who don't wait, who never hesitate to claim space, to impose their narrative. I cannot ignore this, nor the fact that I cannot alter any of it. What I can do is act to contribute to a broader effort for change, an anti-colonial effort that has been unfolding through all time and which, in our time, expresses itself in many different modes and assemblies.

As I removed my hard hat after the first encounter with the palace, I thought it might be a good idea to hold on to the hats, offer them to visitors as a symbolic shield against the coloniality that ambushed from every corner. And then I thought how pathetic if this was the only "protection" I could propose against the threat and insult and aggression in those walls. Was there anything you could effectively set against this building? I said aloud. "The program," an ally replied. A dynamic, exploratory, forensic, collaborative, questioning, restituting, transnational program.

There are moments when I wonder if a forum in a palace might constitute some kind of occupy movement, a group of clandestine political iconoclasts, metaphorically pulling down statues, literally returning belongings, through de-colonial practices. I picture the body builder with knees shaking, arms trembling, on the verge of collapse as these counter forces weigh it down. It remains to be seen if a forum can offer a meaningful passageway from what should not have come to pass.

The palace—packed with your-my-our belongings—is there. If we are to break this colonial lock, many, many more of us need to find, make and share keys.

1 *Stolpersteine*: Brass-plated plaques set into the pavement to commemorate victims of the Third Reich. Started by the artist Gunter Demnig in Germany in 1992, the plaques now extend across Europe, marking the last spot where Jewish and other victims lived or worked before their persecution or extermination by the Nazis and fascist collaborators. Over 100,000 Stolpersteine were laid by 2023; they form the world's most decentralized memorial. | **2** Priyamvada Gopal, *Insurgent Empire: Anti-colonial Resistance and British Dissent* (London/New York: Verso Books, 2019), Epilogue, p. 450. | **3** Donna Haraway, quote from: https://time-issues.org/haraway-statements-on-decolonizing-time/ (accessed April 23, 2025). | **4** Ariella Aisha Azoulay, *Potential History, Unlearning Imperialism* (London/New York: Verso Books, 2019), p. 12. | **5** Ibid. | **6** Dan Hicks, *The Brutish Museums: The Benin Bronzes, Colonial Violence and Cultural Restitution* (London: Pluto Press, 2020), p. vii.

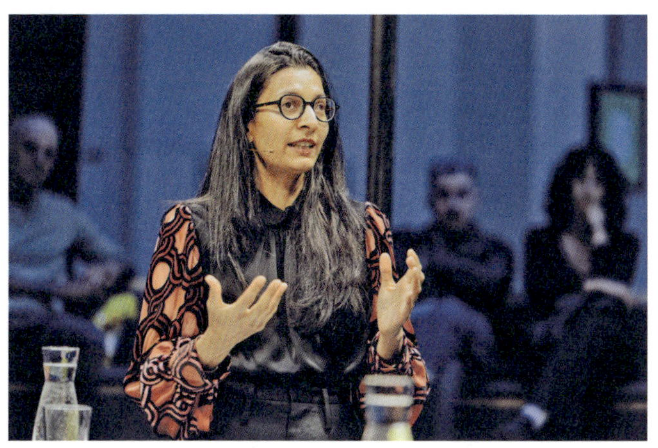

Priya Basil at the Humboldt Forum

OBJECTS
TALK BACK

Meena Kandasamy
A Wise One, a Warrior

Preface by Priya Basil
Paperback, 88 pages

Meena Kandasamy writes about the Mithuna couple, a seventeenth-century ivory sculpture from Tamil Nadu, India, depicting lovers. Kandasamy unfurls a multi-layered, multi-directional narrative built from images, questions and contradictions evoked by the sculpture. "How can we look at this work and not talk about who produced it?" Kandasamy asks and then examines how caste and class are carved into the object as indelibly as its physical details. Such knowledge complicates easy associations of love that may be evoked by the couple.
Refusing any impulse to idealize or exoticize, Kandasamy connects the carving to personal and political stories that expose painful realities of who gets to love whom, and how. She sets the intimate alongside the institutional to interrogate terms such as *decolonize*, *restitution* and *preservation*. Through an astonishing stylistic mix, including Twitter, academic discourse, poetry and memoir, she talks back, forward and sideways with the object.

OBJECTS
TALK BACK

Léonora Miano
Ladies of the Throne

Preface by Priya Basil
Translated from French by Gila Walker
Paperback, 48 pages

"Most of the time, it is the power of men that we remember." With these words, which open Léonora Miano's text for *Objects Talk Back*, an astonishing new narrative unfurls around Mandu Yenu, a throne from the ancient Kingdom of Bamum (present-day Cameroon).

The Germans long claimed the object was a gift from King Njoya to Kaiser Wilhelm II. Miano reads "between the lines of beads and cowrie shells" to show the complex intricacies of colonial and gender relations. Dismissing all pretense of egalitarianism between colonizer and colonized, she hones in on the very nature of power—how and by whom it is defined-wielded-subverted.

King Njoya said he "felt like a woman in his relationship with the Germans." Miano takes this as a prompt to examine contrasting cultural notions of femininity and thus reveals how central women are to the story of the throne. As the very name of the object suggests, it is the power of women we should remember.

OBJECTS
TALK BACK

Rawi Hage
The Call

Preface by Priya Basil
Paperback, 48 pages

After one of the Turfan archaeological expeditions in the early 1900s, a fragment of a Manichaean text written in Uyghur and Old Turkic found its way to the Museum für Asiatische Kunst of the Staatliche Museen zu Berlin. Originating from the Northern Silk Road region (now the Xinjiang Uyghur Autonomous Region in China), these "loose leaves" became a source of inspiration for Rawi Hage: "I was born near Byblos in Lebanon. The ancient city of Byblos is believed to be the place where the first alphabet was invented." Encountering this rare and precious manuscript, with its layered and multicolour words, Hage reflects on the movement, uprooting, displacement and migration of both objects and people.

OBJECTS
TALK BACK

Madeleine Thien
The Artisans

Preface by Priya Basil
Paperback, 48 pages

Canadian writer Madeleine Thien reflects on a fragment of a mural depicting *Three Uyghur Princes* from one of the Bezeklik Caves along the Northern Silk Road, in what is now the Xinjiang Uyghur Autonomous Region of China. This most renowned donor portrait of Uyghur-Buddhist art was brought to the Berlin museums following the Second German Turfan Expedition (1904–5). Thien responds to its vibrant colours and expressive lines with a literary text, transporting us into the daily lives of the painters who adorned the caves with strikingly lifelike murals in the tenth century. She asks: Is there an autonomous republic of art that transcends time and place?

Published by Stiftung Humboldt Forum im Berliner Schloss
General Director: Hartmut Dorgerloh

Concept: Priya Basil
Project management: Katharina Kepplinger
Coordination and text editing: Susanne Müller-Wolff
Image editing: Barbara Martinkat

Special thanks to Lavinia Frey as well as to Fränze Czaja, Philipp Hochleichter, Jan Linders and the staff of the Stiftung Humboldt Forum im Berliner Schloss.

Image p. 5: © SHF, photo: Andreas König, p. 43: © SHF, photo: Johannes Berger

www.humboldtforum.org

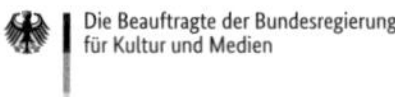

Funded by the Federal Government Commissioner for Culture and the Media in line with a resolution by the German Federal Parliament

External links contained in the text could be reviewed only up to the publication date. The issuer and publisher have had no influence on later changes and can therefore accept no liability. The Deutsche Nationalbibliothek lists this publication in the Deutsche Nationalbibliografie; detailed bibliographic data are available on the Internet at http://dnb.dnb.de.

ISBN 978-3-0358-0752-3
Layout: 2edit, Zurich
Printing: Druckerei Vogl, Zorneding

DIAPHANES – Schöneggstrasse 5 – CH-8004 Zurich
DIAPHANES Berlin – Dresdener Strasse 118 – 10999 Berlin – kontakt@diaphanes.net